D1530588

The French and Indian War

By Hollie Laager

Content Advisor:
Richard J. Bell
History Department
Harvard University

EVENTS IN AMERICAN HISTORY

Rourke
Publishing LLC
Vero Beach, Florida 32964

www.rourkepublishing.com

Image Credits:
Library of Congress, cover (top right and left, bottom right), 1, 4, 6, 10, 12, 13, 18, 26, 27, 29, 30, 31, 34–35, 36–37, 39, 43, 44 (first, second and fourth), 45 (first, second and third), 46 (third, fourth and sixth in first column, second column); North Wind Picture Archives, 9, 22–23; Stock Montage, 6, 14–15, 17, 20, 25, 33, 38, 41, 45 (bottom), 46 (first and second in first column); iStockphoto, cover (bottom left), 5

Editorial Direction: Red Line Editorial, Inc.; Bob Temple

Editor: Nadia Higgins

Designer: Lindaanne Donohoe

Fact Research: Laurie Kahn

Library of Congress Cataloging-in-Publication Data

Laager, Hollie.
    The French and Indian War / by Hollie Laager.
        p. cm. — (Events in American history)
    Includes bibliographical references and index.
    ISBN 1–60044–131–9 (hardcover)
    ISBN 978-1-60044-357-2 (paperback)
    1. United States—History—French and Indian War, 1755–1763—Juvenile literature. I. Title.
    E199.L22 2007
    973.2'6—dc22

                                            2006018725

Printed in the USA

Rourke
Publishing LLC
Vero Beach, Florida 32964

Table of Contents

Chapter One

George Washington Surrenders

y 1753, tensions between the French and the British had reached a breaking point. Both European powers controlled land in North America. The British ruled the colonies along the east coast. West of the colonies, the French were looking to expand their fur-trade empire, exchanging guns and other items with American Indians in return for valuable pelts.

Animal furs were sent back to Europe to make expensive hats and coats.

Great Britain also profited from the fur trade. On and off, Britain and France had been fighting over land and trade since 1689. Now both countries claimed land in the Ohio Valley. For the fourth time in 65 years, war looked likely.

Robert Dinwiddie

"I must desire you to acquaint me by whose authority and instructions you have lately … invaded the King of Great Britain's territories. … It becomes my duty to require your peaceable departure."

From Virginia governor Robert Dinwiddie's letter to the French, delivered by George Washington in 1753

"As to the summons you send me … I do not think myself obliged to obey it."

From the French officer's response to Governor Dinwiddie's demands

According to the British, the Ohio Valley fell within the boundaries of their Virginia colony. In the fall of 1753, Virginia governor Robert Dinwiddie sent a young military officer named George Washington to deliver a letter to the French, warning them to stop building forts in the Ohio Valley and to vacate the ones already there. This dangerous mission was one of Washington's first. The future president of the United States was just 21 and spoke little French. However, he was eager to prove himself worthy of the challenge.

*George Washington rode through the wilderness of the Ohio Valley
to deliver a warning letter to the French.*

With a translator and a few local woodsmen, Washington headed into the wilderness. He delivered the message to a French commander, who was not worried by the letter's threats. Upon his return to Virginia, Washington reported both on France's refusal and on the alarming strength of its forts, weapons, and soldiers in the Ohio Valley. Although the young officer had never before seen battle, he was made lieutenant colonel and sent back into the area with 150 soldiers at his command.

Washington's men first attacked the French on May 28, 1754, just a few miles from the British camp at Great Meadows. In the hours before dawn, the Virginians surrounded the French, killing several men and capturing many others. Following this battle, Washington and his men built a small fort, which they called Fort Necessity.

Fort Necessity was little more than a stockade of logs when the French attacked it about a month after their initial skirmish with Washington. The French, far outnumbering the Virginians, succeeded in trapping the young commander and his men in the fort.

"We formed ourselves for an Engagement, marching one after the other, in the Indian Manner: We were advanced pretty near to [the French] ... when they discovered us; whereupon I ordered my Company to fire. [The battle] only lasted a Quarter of an Hour, before the Enemy was routed."

George Washington describing the May 28, 1754, battle in his diary

Inside, food supplies were dangerously low, and a rainstorm earlier that day had completely soaked their ammunition.

Nearly one-third of the Virginians were killed. Soon Washington realized his only hope of survival was to surrender. The French allowed Washington to retreat only after he agreed to leave two of his officers behind as hostages. Then he and his troops headed back to Virginia in defeat. This one-day battle is often regarded as the unofficial start of the French and Indian War.

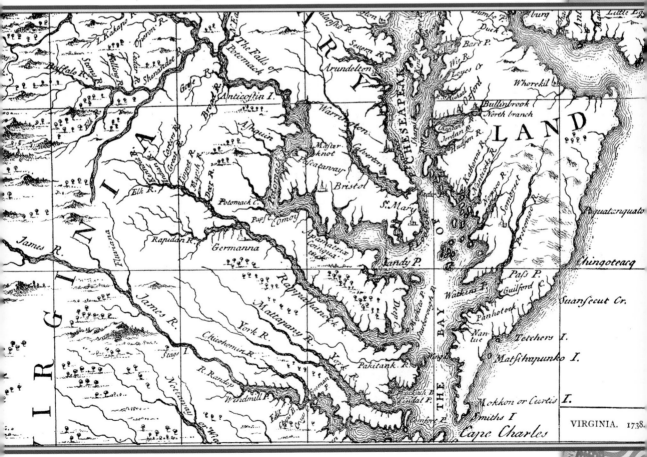

A historic map shows what it calls "Virginia Land." The first Americans to fight in the French and Indian War were from the Virginia colony, which bordered disputed land in the Ohio Valley.

Chapter Two

Heading Toward Conflict

In the seventeenth century, the United States did not yet exist. Until Columbus made land in 1492, North America's only inhabitants had been American Indians. Over the next two centuries, however, European explorers had been arriving in the New World, each claiming territory for its rulers. Sections of the continent were now controlled by such distant European countries as Holland, Spain, Sweden, France, and Great Britain. Citizens from these countries traveled to the New World to build settlements and find their fortunes. One of the first French settlements was Quebec, Canada, which served mainly as a trading center. The first successful British colony was Jamestown, Virginia, settled in 1607.

In Europe and Canada, the French and Indian War came to be known as the Seven Years War. "Seven Years" refers to the length of the war from the time it was officially declared in May 1756.

Opposite page: English settlers trade with American Indians at a British colony.

Throughout the seventeenth century, France continued to take control of eastern Canada. Swedish and Dutch colonies centered around New York, while British colonies lined the Atlantic coast from Georgia to Maine. Eventually, Great Britain pushed Sweden and Holland out of the area, claiming the land as its own and establishing itself as France's major rival for the eastern half of North America. Competition for land and trade led them to war three times between the years 1689 and 1748. By 1750, the fourth and last of such wars was about to break out.

Europeans relied on trade with American Indians in North America.

Once again, both Britain and France were looking to expand their settlements. New conflicts over trade had arisen as well. And differences over religion were also causing bad feeling between the groups. Most French were Catholic, while the British were Protestant.

By now, the French claimed land that ranged from the Great Lakes in the north to Louisiana in the south. Communities, trading posts, and forts sprang up in order to help France protect its land. Detroit, New Orleans, Montreal, and Quebec were all under French control.

In the 1700s, France controlled Quebec, located along the St. Lawrence River in eastern Canada.

Trade with Indians

The Indians of North America had been trading items such as corn, squash, animal skins, and meat with each other for centuries. With the Europeans' arrival, however, this way of life was forever changed. Indians provided the settlers with furs that brought in a great deal of money back in Europe. In return, the settlers supplied such items as cloth, jewelry, beads, ammunition, hatchets, and guns—goods the Indians came to rely on.

Meanwhile, local Indians continued doing business with the French, who had a reputation for trading fairly with them. The Iroquois Confederacy, which was made up of several Indian nations, held claim to the land located between the French and British colonies. Eventually, British traders moved into the Ohio area and began trading with the Indians as

well. Very soon, the struggle for power and land between these three groups would erupt in war.

In 1749, the British king granted a large plot of land in the Ohio Valley to a group of Virginia businessmen. France, however, had claimed the same land earlier that year. To keep the British from moving farther into the valley, the French began to build more forts there. Great Britain, hoping to strengthen its hold on the territory, retaliated by constructing forts of its own.

Iroquois Indians are known for their dwellings, called longhouses. The Indians controlled the fur trade in present-day New York state and beyond. During the French and Indian War, they sided with the British.

When he was sent by Governor Dinwiddie to deliver the warning to the French in 1753, Washington discovered a spot that was ideal for a fort. The following spring, Dinwiddie ordered the construction of a fort where the Monongahela and Allegheny Rivers meet—exactly as Washington had suggested.

Fort Duquesne was located in present-day Pittsburgh. It had actually been renamed Fort Pitt, and the city of Pittsburgh grew around it over time. During the course of the war, Fort Duquesne would change hands—and names—many times. It was a key fort in the French and Indian War.

The young George Washington had never before faced combat in 1753. And yet he was sent in command of a dangerous military expedition to confront the French.

During the fort's construction, however, a much larger French troop forced the British to retreat and took over the structure, renaming it Fort Duquesne. Washington and his men were forced to set up a small, makeshift stockade nearby, which they called Fort Necessity. The battle that ensued there, in July 1754, was the unofficial start of the French and Indian War.

Chapter Three

The Beginning of the War

In early 1755, General Edward Braddock was put in charge of the British troops in America. At this time, war still had not been officially declared by the French or the British. Braddock's task was to take over the French-controlled Fort Duquesne.

Accompanied by George Washington and his men, Braddock's army of 1,400 soldiers marched toward the fort. A 4-mile (6.4-kilometer) column of soldiers traveled slowly through the dense forest. Because they had to clear a path with axes as they went, they covered just a few miles each day.

Along the way, an opposition force of around 850 French, Canadian, and Indian soldiers attacked the expedition from all sides. Braddock's men were completely surprised, and most of them panicked. Though they outnumbered the French, the British suffered an overwhelming defeat. They lost more than 900 men, including Braddock himself.

"These savages may indeed be a formidable enemy to raw American military, but upon the king's regular and disciplined troops, sir, it is impossible they should make an impression."

General Edward Braddock, responding to Benjamin Franklin, who predicted that taking Fort Duquesne would not be as easy as the general believed. Braddock ignored similar warnings from George Washington.

One of the problems for the British was the way in which they fought. British armies were used to lining up in orderly rows, a technique that had worked well in the open battlefields of Europe. The French and Indians fought much differently, firing at the British while hiding behind rocks and trees. This method proved to be much more effective in the woods of the Ohio Valley.

The defeat hurt the English in another way. Indians had already established closer ties to the French than to the British. Now they were eager to side with the winners. After this battle, Indians were primarily fighting on the side of the French.

Farther north, however, things were going better for the British. They built two new forts, Fort Edward, on the Hudson River, and Fort William Henry, on the southern end of Lake George. The British also defeated the French at Lake George in June 1755, enabling them to take over Fort Beauséjour in Nova Scotia.

"The Virginia companies behaved like men and died like soldiers; for I believe out of three companies that were on the ground that day scarce thirty were left alive."

George Washington to Governor Robert Dinwiddie, in his written account of the defeat of Edward Braddock, July 9, 1755

An illustration from the late 1700s depicts a bloody battle from the French and Indian War.

After their victory in Nova Scotia, the British deported, or kicked out, more than six thousand French-speaking residents, known as Acadians. The British worried that the Acadians would remain loyal to France and act as spies. This only increased hatred between the French and the British, however.

After Acadians refused to pledge loyalty to the British king, the British forced the French-speaking colonists out of their homes in Nova Scotia.

A Shift in Control

In 1757, the British leader William Pitt began to turn things around for his country. Pitt believed that the way to defeat the French was to attack them not only in North America, but also around the world, in places such as India and the West Indies.

But the American colonists were unhappy about Pitt's new rules. He wanted the Americans to pitch in for the war effort, forcing them to supply equipment, shelter, and manpower. Colonists resisted these orders, sometimes violently.

William Pitt

William Pitt

Known for his outspokenness and passion, William Pitt had a stormy career in public office. He is remembered for both dazzling success and dismal failure. In 1755, just three years before his victories in the French and Indian War, Pitt had been fired from his position with the British military for speaking out against his superior, the Duke of Newcastle. Pitt was reinstated just one year later, after Newcastle fell from power. In 1757, Pitt was forced from office once again—only to make a comeback within the year.

In the 1760s, after retiring from the military, Pitt spoke out against unpopular British policies in the American colonies. Pitt was already well-known in America for his role in the French and Indian War. Now his fame skyrocketed.

Eventually Pitt rose to the position of prime minister of Great Britain. However, he proved to be a much more capable military leader than political one. He resigned from office in October 1768 in ill health, never to return to public office. Until his death, in 1778, Pitt continued to speak out with great feeling and frankness about the controversies of his day.

This tension between the British military and the colonists almost interrupted the war. In 1758, responding to American protests, Pitt softened the rules. Immediately, American support for the war and the number of recruits increased. By now, the British far outnumbered the French. But that was only one of the problems facing France, which was having trouble providing food for its soldiers.

In 1758, Pitt made what proved to be key decisions in the war. First he instructed the British navy to block the passage of French fleets at sea. This made it safer for British soldiers and supplies to be sent to America. Another crucial move by Pitt was to bring two important figures into the war, generals Jeffrey Amherst and James Wolfe.

"I thank thee, Pitt, for all thy glorious strife against the foes of LIBERTY and life."

Unknown author, expressing a common sentiment in the colonies after the many victories of 1758. Many ships and even some towns were named after Pitt during this period.

Above: Jeffrey Amherst
Left: James Wolfe

A 1759 drawing shows Fort Ticonderoga amid the wilderness of northeastern New York.

Then, with thousands of British troops in place, Pitt ordered an attack on Canada. In July, General James Abercrombie led some fifteen thousand colonial and British troops north from Albany to Montreal. The march was halted by French forces in northeastern New York at Fort Carillon (later called Fort Ticonderoga). But the British would soon recover with three important victories.

A month before Abercrombie's defeat, more than fourteen thousand British troops under the direction of generals Jeffrey Amherst and James Wolfe had laid siege to the fortress of Louisbourg, near the mouth of the St. Lawrence River. Forty-eight days later, the French surrendered this strategic location to Great Britain.

In the distance, British warships approach Louisbourg.

"By this Event, France is deprived of the Key to her North American Trade, and of the Means to insult and encroach upon our Settlements."

From a piece in the Pennsylvania Gazette about the fall of Louisbourg to British forces

The next British victory was at Fort Frontenac, on Lake Ontario. Frontenac had been France's principal supply center. Without it, there was no way for them to bring food, weapons, or even troops into the area. The French forces were paralyzed.

Then about six thousand British soldiers moved in on the French-controlled Fort Duquesne. This attack was led by General John Forbes, along with George Washington. Initially, the French seemed to be in charge. After two months, however, Fort Duquesne fell under British control. Much of the fort was destroyed by the French before they left. The British rebuilt the fort, renaming it Fort Pitt, in honor of William Pitt.

During this time, Pitt also held meetings with the Indian tribes and finally was able to make peace between the British and the Indians. Though this peace would not last long, the French had lost a powerful ally. For the first time since war broke out, the British controlled the Ohio Valley.

George Washington (on the white horse) lifts his hat as a British flag is raised at Fort Duquesne in 1758.

Chapter Five

Final Victories and Effects of the War

The year 1759 showed no letup by the British, who had captured fort after fort from the French. These victories led William Pitt to continue the strike against Canada at full force. Pitt made Jeffrey Amherst commander-in-chief of the British army. Amherst and his men proceeded to take control of two more French forts, Fort Carillon (Ticonderoga) and Crown Point.

With a victory over Montreal (shown here), Great Britain effectively won the French and Indian War in 1760.

EVENTS IN AMERICAN HISTORY

That summer, Fort Niagara was also captured under Amherst's leadership. Situated where Lakes Ontario and Erie meet, Niagara was an important victory for the British, forcing the French to retreat further.

But the British were not yet finished. They knew that capturing the city of Quebec would cripple the French. But it would not be easy: Sitting atop steep cliffs overlooking the St. Lawrence River, Quebec was France's most secure stronghold.

Quebec stood on high bluffs along the St. Lawrence River.

In June 1759, the British embarked on the most ambitious attack of the war to that point. General James Wolfe led a force of about nine thousand soldiers. For months, the British fired at Quebec from below the city. But the French, under Montcalm's leadership, stayed protected behind the fort's walls. Montcalm hoped to keep the British at bay until winter, when the river would ice over and Wolfe would be forced to retreat. How could Wolfe get the French troops out into the open for battle before then?

Prior to the attack in 1759, the British had twice tried—and failed—to capture Quebec. This led the French to believe their fort to be unconquerable.

Finally, in September, Wolfe found a path to the city that was not well guarded. Under cover of darkness, more than four thousand of his men climbed the steep cliffs and gathered on a field outside the walls. In the morning, they surprised the French, who had no choice but to come out and battle.

After just 15 minutes under heavy fire, the French surrendered. Montcalm himself was badly wounded and would die the following day. The British suffered a great loss, too. General James Wolfe was killed during this battle.

Before Wolfe came up with a plan to attack Quebec, his army had been on the brink of crisis. More than one-third of his men were ill with a serious fever. Those healthy enough to fight were deserting the army in high numbers.

In this artistic portrayal, General James Wolfe dies in the arms of fellow soldiers during the Battle of Quebec.

With Wolfe gone, Amherst continued the march toward Montreal. On September 8, 1760, one year after the loss of Quebec, the French surrendered the city of Montreal to the British. Great Britain now had won complete control of North America from the French. Though small battles would continue for the next few years, the British had effectively won the war. The official end came with the signing of the Treaty of Paris on February 10, 1763. Canada and all of North America east of the Mississippi River, with the exception of New Orleans, went to the British.

"There shall be a Christian, universal, and perpetual peace. ... [The] parties shall give the greatest attention to maintain [friendship] between themselves ... without permitting, on either side, any kind of hostilities, by sea or by land, to be committed from henceforth, for any cause."

The Treaty of Paris, 1763

The Treaty of Paris

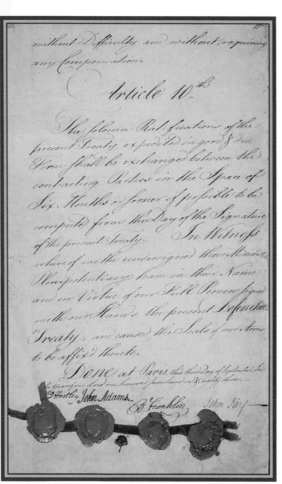

Pontiac's Rebellion

Pontiac had fought on the side of the French during the French and Indian War. However, he believed that American Indians—not France or Great Britain—held the true land claim to the Ohio Valley and other land west of the Allegheny Mountains. In 1763, Pontiac formed an alliance of Indian tribes to battle the British. With promises of French support, he led attacks against British forts in the Detroit area, capturing eight of them. The British held on to other key forts, however, and after several months, the Indians were running out of guns and ammunition. The help they were expecting from the French never came, and Pontiac was forced to give up.

After Pontiac's Rebellion, Great Britain wanted to avoid further costly wars with natives. The British Royal Proclamation of 1763 made it illegal for colonists to settle west of the Allegheny Mountains. The proclamation had little effect, however, and was mostly ignored by settlers eager for new land out west.

"We now have the Pleasure to congratulate our Countrymen upon the most important Event ... the War in Canada is at an End: The Governor, has surrendered the Country to the British General Amherst without Bloodshed. The Subjects of France are to be sent Home, all that remain of the French are to swear Allegiance to His Majesty."

The Pennsylvania Gazette, regarding the fall of Montreal to the British in 1760

Even after the treaty was signed, some fighting continued, but this time the Indians fought the British alone. Pontiac, who had been a French ally, led some successful attacks against British forts but was soon defeated. Indian relations with the British would become increasingly strained. Fighting over land and rights would continue for years. The French and Indian War had lasting effects on relations between Great Britain and the American colonies.

Britain was disappointed with the Americans. They felt that the colonists had not supported the war enough—a war, as the British saw it, that was for the Americans' own protection. Also, during this war, many American merchants had traded illegally with the French. Some had even traded with the French troops, providing them with the food and supplies that the British had worked so hard to keep from them.

The government of Great Britain had gone into debt to pay for the war in North America. Because most of the war had been fought on American soil, and because it was to secure the colonies' lands, the British felt it was only fair to make the colonists repay this debt. So the British imposed new taxes on the Americans. This taxation did not sit well with the colonists and, in fact, was one of the issues that led to the American Revolution.

A 1772 map shows British-controlled land in North America (all colored areas) after the French and Indian War.

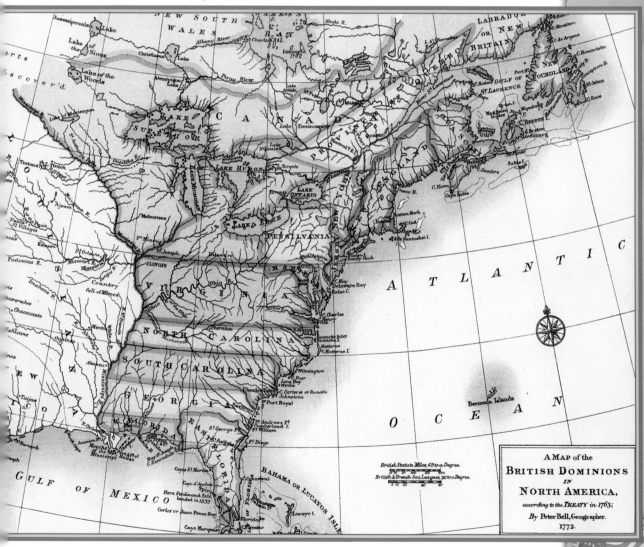

Many British troops stayed on in North America after the French and Indian War. The continued presence of the soldiers made the Americans uneasy. With the increased demands by the British government, the colonists began to actively resist the troops. Encounters between Americans and British forces soon turned violent. By 1775, the American Revolution was under way. In this way, the French and Indian War led not only to Great Britain's takeover of French land in North America, but also to the birth of the United States.

Some 20 years after his role in the French and Indian War, George Washington achieved great fame as a leader of the American Revolution.

Biographies

Jeffrey Amherst (1717–97)

An important British general during the war, Jeffrey Amherst led the assault on Louisbourg and other key battles. He also helped capture Montreal, the final French city to fall. Following the war, Amherst was appointed governor-general of British North America.

Edward Braddock (ca. 1695–1755)

Edward Braddock was in charge of the British troops early on, before war had officially been declared. His mission was to capture the French Fort Duquesne. Many men died in this battle, including Braddock.

Robert Dinwiddie (1693–1770)

Robert Dinwiddie served as governor of Virginia from 1751 to 1758, when it was still a British colony. In late 1753, Dinwiddie sent a young George Washington on an expedition to tell the French to leave the Ohio Valley. He later sent General Edward Braddock and his troops to Virginia.

Louis-Joseph de Montcalm (1712–59)

Louis-Joseph de Montcalm was the commander of French troops in North America. Though he led many French victories during the early stages of the war, Montcalm is best remembered for his defeat at Quebec in 1759. He was wounded during this decisive battle and died the next day.

William Pitt (1708–78)

William Pitt is credited with turning the fortunes of the British in the French and Indian War. He brought many key figures into the war and was the driving force behind attacking France around the world. His strategies resulted in many British victories, and Pitt became an enormously popular figure both in the British government and the American colonies.

Pontiac (ca. 1720–69)

Probably born in northern Ohio, Pontiac was a leader of the Ottawa tribe and fought on the side of the French during the French and Indian War. Afterward, he formed an alliance of Indian tribes to fight British control of land west of the Allegheny Mountains. In addition to being a warrior, Pontiac was a priest of a religious group called the Grand Medicine Society. Pontiac came to believe that Indians should stop all trade with white people.

George Washington (1732–99)

George Washington is remembered as being a Revolutionary War hero and the first president of the United States (1789–97), but he got his start in the British military. Washington's defeat at Fort Necessity was the first battle of the French and Indian War.

James Wolfe (1727–59)

Selected by William Pitt to aid the British in the war efforts, James Wolfe was named second–in-command to Jeffrey Amherst. Together, Amherst and Wolfe won many battles and captured important forts and cities for the British. Wolfe is best remembered for leading the attack at Quebec, effectively securing a British victory in the war. He was killed in the famous battle.

Timeline

July 3, 1754
George Washington and his men surrender at Fort Necessity.

1754

June 1755
After nearly two weeks of fighting, British troops take control of Fort Beauséjour.

July 9, 1755
Edward Braddock and his troops are defeated at Fort Duquesne. Braddock dies a few days later from injuries received in battle.

May 1756
Great Britain officially declares war on France.

August 14, 1756
British troops surrender at Fort Oswego.

August 9, 1757
The French capture Fort William Henry.

July 26, 1759
Fort Niagara falls to the British.

September 13, 1759
British forces take control of Quebec.

September 8, 1760
Montreal is captured by the British.

1763

February 10, 1763
The Treaty of Paris is signed, officially ending the war.

Glossary

ammunition (AM-u-NISH-uhn)
a supply of bullets, cannonballs, and other items that are fired from weapons such as guns

capture (KAP-shuhr)
to take control of something that once belonged to someone else

colony (KOL-uh-nee)
a group of people who settle in a distant land while remaining citizens of their original country; also the word for the place they settle

debt (DEHT)
owing money

empire (EHM-pyr)
a huge operation, such as a business, controlled by just one person or group

grenade (grah-NAYD)
a small bomb that is thrown by hand

hatchet (HACH-it)
a small, short ax designed to be used with just one hand

hostage (HOS-tihj)
a person who is kidnapped in order to force a group, such as a country, to meet a condition; in war, hostages are often held until the war is over

retreat (rih-TREET)
to back away from a battle or other difficult situation

strategic (stra-TEE-jihk)
well-planned; playing a key part

taxation (taks-AY-shun)
the act of charging a tax, which is money the government charges its citizens to pay for for wars and other national expenses

Further Resources

Web Links

Infoplease: The French and Indian War
www.infoplease.com/ce6/history/A0858256.html
This Web site contains information on the war from beginning to end.

Social Studies for Kids: The French and Indian War
www.socialstudiesforkids.com/wwww/us/frenchandindianwardef.htm
This Web site provides an overview of the French and Indian War for students. It breaks down and easily organizes the events of the war.

SparkNotes: The French and Indian War
www.sparknotes.com/history/american/frenchindian
Students select the portion of the war they are looking for, and the information is provided for all parts of the battle.

Books

Maestro, Betsy. *Struggle for a Continent: The French and Indian Wars, 1689–1763.* HarperCollins, 2000.

Smolinski, Diane. *Battles of the French and Indian War.* Heinemann Library, 2003.

Todish, Timothy J. *America's First First World War: The French and Indian War, 1754–1763.* Purple Mountain Press, 2002.

Index